Save the Day

APPLYING GOD'S WISDOM TO LIFE'S STRUGGLES

TERRIE CHAPPELL

First published in 2015 by Striving Together Publications, a ministry
of Lancaster Baptist Church, Lancaster, CA 93535. Striving Together
Publications is committed to providing tried, trusted, and proven
resources that will further equip local churches to carry out the
Great Commission. Your comments and suggestions are valued.

Striving Together Publications
4020 E. Lancaster Blvd.
Lancaster, CA 93535
800.201.7748
strivingtogether.com

Cover design by Andrew Jones
Layout by Craig Parker
Writing assistance by Danielle Mordh
Special thanks to our proofreaders

The author and publication team have put forth every effort to give proper
credit to quotes and thoughts that are not original with the author. It is not
our intent to claim originality with any quote or thought that could not
readily be tied to an original source.

ISBN 978-1-59894-297-2
Printed in the United States of America

CONTENTS

Introduction
When Folly Reigns   v

Chapter One
The Circumstances of a Wise Woman   1

Chapter Two
The Cry of a Wise Woman   15

Chapter Three
The Communication of a Wise Woman   25

Chapter Four
The Courage of a Wise Woman   37

Chapter Five
The Choices of a Wise Woman   45

Conclusion
When Wisdom Abounds   55

When Folly Reigns

I'll never forget my first Sunday of ministry as an assistant pastor's wife in Northern California. My husband and I had served in various capacities leading up to this time, but this position was new for us, and we were excited to jump in and help in any way we could. For me, that meant teaching the three-year-old's class on our first Sunday morning.

I enjoy teaching children and had a great morning of Sunday school perfectly planned for those precious three-year-olds. I had a song list, Bible story, schedule, snack, and system all in place. The one thing I did not have was a helper.

My husband, who was the new children's ministry director, pulled all my helpers to work in other classrooms, and I found myself standing in a room of adorable (and hyper) three-year-old boys and girls. Still, I was determined to have a good morning. After all, this was our new ministry, and I wanted to serve the Lord with gladness and efficiency while making our pastor and his wife thankful they chose to bring my husband and me on the team.

So, I pressed forward. We sang songs, and that went great. I told a Bible story, and they listened as well as could be expected. But then, someone had to go potty. And as it usually goes with three-year-olds, *everyone* had to go potty.

I quickly formulated a plan. The ladies restroom down the hall had a lounge that was separate from the stalls and sinks. I would have the boys sit in the lounge while I helped the girls in the restroom, and then we would switch. I would help the boys in the restroom while the girls sat peacefully in the lounge until we finished.

As I took the girls to the restroom, the boys were doing pretty well—at least staying contained in the lounge area—and I was feeling proud of my problem solving and quick thinking.

And then we switched—boys in the restroom and girls in the lounge. The girls, however, decided this was the cue that they could go back to class. Before I knew it, they were running and twirling their beautiful Sunday dresses down the church halls headed toward the classroom.

Worried that they might run out the front doors or encounter some other harm, I ran out of the ladies restroom to gather them. The ushers helped me with the girls who ran down the hall, and I ran to the classroom to get the ones who went there. But I couldn't get in. Those sweet three-year-old girls had locked me out of the classroom. I stood, looking through the window, as they took out the toys, ate the snacks, and practically gave me a heart attack.

While the ushers helped me unlock the classroom, I ran back to the ladies restroom where I found the boys had taken full reign. They were having the time of their lives—standing in the toilets and in the sinks, playing with the toilet paper, and having water fights.

I stood there in a moment of discouragement and dismay and thought to myself, "This is out of control! Where is the wisdom in this?!"

I had started my day ready to serve the Lord. I had prepared and tried to keep a good spirit. I had done my best, but this was chaos. Despite my best efforts and quick thinking, I needed real wisdom to bring calm and order to the situation. The three-year-olds had taken control in all of their adorable folly, and I was desperately seeking for a wise solution to handle the circumstance at hand.

This incident is but a microcosm of the folly that reigns in our society today. It seems that everywhere you turn, people are doing right in their own eyes. Society is out of control, and sin is running rampant. Perhaps even in your own life you have been frustrated by the results of your wrong choices and lack of wisdom. I know I have been.

When I have days that feel like a rerun of the three-year-old takeover, I really like to hear from women who identify with me—women who have similar stories that let me know I'm not the only one to experience crazy situations like this. I suppose that's why I love the story of an unnamed wise woman in 2 Samuel 20. This story is encouraging to me because in her day as well folly reigned. There was a lack of wisdom, and it wasn't just among the three-year-olds and their teachers! Even among the good leaders in the land, wisdom was wanting. Yet this woman obtained God-given wisdom to deal with the problems she faced.

If you can identify with the frustrations that accompany folly, join me as we study the wise responses of this unnamed woman. From this passage, we can gain a better understanding of exactly what happens when there is a lack of wisdom in our lives and how we can apply God's wisdom even in desperately out-of-control situations.

CHAPTER ONE

The Circumstances of a Wise Woman

If you're like me, you've noticed that life is full of problems. Who *doesn't* face them? Some problems are large and alter the course of our lives. Some problems are small, and we feel confident that we can face them alone. Whether large or small, problems will find us wherever we go and in whatever life stage. In fact, the natural course of life is that we either just had a problem, are having a problem, or will have a problem.

I think it is safe to say that we as women have two things in common regarding problems: first, we all face them. No one is exempt—not the experienced mom, the inexperienced bride, nor the confident single. None of us escapes the struggles of life.

The second common factor is that we can all obtain wisdom. It is available to everyone. Actually, life's problems offer perfect opportunities to exercise wisdom.

Sometimes we look at someone who seems to "have it all together," and we assume she does not face any problems. The fact is, she faces problems. But if her appearance of serenity is real, it is because she has learned to exercise wisdom in the face of problems.

The wise woman of 2 Samuel 20 had her share of problems. She was caught in the middle of and suffering for other people's unwise choices, yet she exercised an incredibly perceptive degree of wisdom that changed an entire situation.

To understand her response, however, we have to first understand the background of her situation. What does a takeover of folly look like? Notice these aspects that set the scene for our wise woman, and consider how these may be playing out in your circumstances as well:

The Devil Fights

And there happened to be there a man of Belial, whose name was Sheba, the son of Bichri, a Benjamite: and he blew a trumpet, and said, We have no part in David, neither have we inheritance in the son of Jesse: every man to his tents, O Israel. So every man of Israel went up from after David, and followed Sheba the son of Bichri: but the men of Judah clave unto their king, from Jordan even to Jerusalem.

—2 SAMUEL 20:1–2

The first verse of 2 Samuel 20 introduces us to Sheba. He was the son of Bichri, a Benjamite, and he caused a rebellion against King David while heading north through all the tribes of Israel, gathering recruits along the way.

The setting for this moment is David returning to Jerusalem after his son Absalom's rebellion and political takeover. Many years ago, a preacher by the name of John Trapp observed, "The devil loves to fish in troubled waters." That was certainly true at this moment in King David's life. In the wake of one difficulty, another came crashing in. No sooner had David crossed the Jordan River to return to Jerusalem, than Sheba led a new wave of rebellion.

As a "son of Belial," Sheba was a personification of all that is evil. The Bible says that he blew a trumpet to get the attention of others and to declare his rivalry with David. The sad part? The men of Israel left David and followed Sheba. Only the tribe of Judah remained loyal to their king.

As I read these first two verses in our story, I can't help but think about the day that we live in. Our culture is full of wickedness. Evildoers blow their trumpets in blatant defiance of God's ways, rallying people around ungodly causes and wanting no part in God's plan for peace and security. Perhaps even more discouraging is to see people follow these rally cries. It often seems as if everyone in the world around us is forsaking God and walking in the ways of wickedness.

But the devil doesn't only fight in national and cultural arenas. He fights the home too. Perhaps even recently you have been sensing his assault on the lives of those in your home. Maybe your child is listening to the trumpet call of a dangerous friend, leaving the authority of your home to follow a "Sheba" in his life. Maybe a trumpet call is undermining loyalty or faithfulness in your marriage as someone or something is pulling your relationship apart. Maybe trying circumstances are blasting your peace with a trumpet call to worry or fear. The blowing doesn't seem to stop, and neither do the tears or sleepless nights.

In whatever situation you face, remember there is hope because God offers you His wisdom. We'll get to that part soon, but for now, let's uncover another consequence of the lack of wisdom.

Relationships Suffer

*And David came to his house at Jerusalem;
and the king took the ten women his
concubines, whom he had left to keep the
house, and put them in ward, and fed them,
but went not in unto them. So they were
shut up unto the day of their death, living in
widowhood.*—2 SAMUEL 20:3

As David returned home from Absalom's
rebellion just as Sheba was leading a new wave
of rebellion, things were tense at home. The
repercussions of all of this involved tragedy in David's
home relationships—for everyone involved.

When folly abounds in our lives, we too will
suffer from broken and strained relationships. When
life gets crazy, society is wicked, men are frustrated,
and women are hurting—this is when we need God's
wisdom! If you've ever experienced a relational strain
with a family member, spouse, child, or friend, you
can testify to the desperate need we have for wisdom
during these tense and painful circumstances.

Apathy Sets In

Then said the king to Amasa, Assemble me the men of Judah within three days, and be thou here present. So Amasa went to assemble the men of Judah: but he tarried longer than the set time which he had appointed him.

—2 SAMUEL 20:4–5

In response to Sheba's rebellion, David commanded one of his generals, Amasa, to gather all the men of Judah together within three days. David was a decisive leader, and he knew this rebellion could not go unchecked for long. He was preparing for military action, and he had only a short window in which to do it.

Unfortunately, while Amasa seemed to have good intentions, he didn't have good follow through. He didn't seem to share David's sense of urgency.

Perhaps you, like me, often become frustrated with the apathy that is so prevalent in our society. With Christians being persecuted around the world, unborn babies dying in America, and countless other injustices taking place on a daily basis, it seems that more should be passionate about fighting God's battles and standing with Him for truth and right.

Maybe, on a more personal level, you are frustrated with the personal apathy you experience in your own life. Again, if you're like me, you might become discouraged with the lack of consistency in your walk with God. Or your lack of passion to tell others about Him. Or your lack of fervency in raising godly children or nurturing your relationship with your husband. Whatever the case, apathy is a constant struggle for most of us, and it is an indicator that we need God's wisdom to fight it.

Loss Is Inevitable

And David said to Abishai, Now shall Sheba the son of Bichri do us more harm than did Absalom: take thou thy lord's servants, and pursue after him, lest he get him fenced cities, and escape us. And there went out after him Joab's men, and the Cherethites, and the

Pelethites, and all the mighty men: and they went out of Jerusalem, to pursue after Sheba the son of Bichri. When they were at the great stone which is in Gibeon, Amasa went before them. And Joab's garment that he had put on was girded unto him, and upon it a girdle with a sword fastened upon his loins in the sheath thereof; and as he went forth it fell out. And Joab said to Amasa, Art thou in health, my brother? And Joab took Amasa by the beard with the right hand to kiss him. But Amasa took no heed to the sword that was in Joab's hand: so he smote him therewith in the fifth rib, and shed out his bowels to the ground, and struck him not again; and he died. So Joab and Abishai his brother pursued after Sheba the son of Bichri.—2 SAMUEL 20:6–10

When Amasa failed to follow orders, King David became concerned that Amasa's apathy would allow Sheba time to assemble his forces from within the safety of walled cities. David sent Abishai, another of his generals, with the army at hand to pursue Sheba. On the way, they encountered Amasa, who still seemed to be taking his time in fulfilling the king's command.

Abishai's brother, Joab, was no stranger to war and bloodshed. Frustrated by Amasa's disobedience and perhaps motivated by political rivalry, he deceived Amasa by pretending to greet him warmly. Amasa wasn't only lethargic; he was oblivious. He didn't even see the sword Joab had, poised to kill him.

When folly reigns, loss is inevitable. When even well-intentioned people (ourselves included) do not respond to life's challenges with God-given wisdom, we lose. We may lose relationships. We may lose our temper. We may lose our joy. We may lose our sweet spirit. In tragic cases, there may even be the loss of a life, as we see in this passage. When we retain God's wisdom, we retain His blessings. When we ignore His wisdom, spiritual loss is sure to follow.

Distractions Abound

And one of Joab's men stood by him, and said, He that favoureth Joab, and he that is

for David, let him go after Joab. And Amasa
wallowed in blood in the midst of the highway.
And when the man saw that all the people
stood still, he removed Amasa out of the
highway into the field, and cast a cloth upon
him, when he saw that every one that came
by him stood still. When he was removed out
of the highway, all the people went on after
Joab, to pursue after Sheba the son of Bichri.
—2 SAMUEL 20:11–13

Have you ever been stuck in a terrible traffic
jam, only to eventually learn that the cause of the
jam wasn't a road block? It was an accident with the
involved cars now on the shoulder of the road, but
other drivers (perhaps yourself included) are slowing
down out of curiosity, shock, or sadness to take
inventory of the damage.

We find a similar situation in 2 Samuel 20. After
Joab killed Amasa, one of his men rallied the troops
and encouraged them to press forward in battle
against Sheba. The only problem was that Amasa's

body wallowing in blood in the middle of the highway was distracting. As the men encountered his corpse on their charge to fight Sheba, they got distracted and stood still. Maybe they were shocked that Joab had killed him. Maybe they were horrified by the condition of his speared body. Maybe they were saddened by his choice to delay when David asked for haste. Whatever the case, they were distracted. They stood still instead of pressing forward.

Sometimes *we* get distracted by the devastation and loss around us. We read the news constantly, update our social media feeds frequently, and stress continually (perhaps even subconsciously) about the perceived hopelessness that abounds.

God doesn't want us to be distracted in His work. It is His desire that we stay focused on His purposes and remain fully engaged in spiritual battle. Like the man who pulled Amasa's body off the highway, we must remove distractions and press forward in God's wisdom to win God's battles.

Seeking Wisdom

The first thirteen verses of 2 Samuel 20 show me one primary truth: We need wisdom. And if we don't have it, bad stuff happens. Furthermore, when others around us don't have wisdom, bad stuff happens.

I once read a story of a sixty-year-old man who divorced his wife. They decided to split their belongings, including the house. Surprisingly, the man did *exactly* that. He literally split the house in half and gave half of his house to his wife, keeping the rest for himself. Even sixty years of life experience hadn't convinced him better.

Truly, wisdom can escape us at any point in life, and it's desperately missed when it's gone. No matter how old you are, how much education you have, how many experiences you have faced in life, you need wisdom today.

I want God's wisdom. I don't want folly to reign in my life, resulting in loss, distraction, and apathy. When I find myself in situations where folly does reign, I want to be able to respond in godly wisdom to turn the tide of danger and destruction.

CHAPTER TWO

The Cry of a Wise Woman

The scene isn't pretty. Sheba is rebelling. Amasa has been killed. Emotions are high. Leaders are passionate. People are angry. Folly abounds.

Through all of this, Sheba is escaping, assembling an army on the move. If he could reach a walled city, he would be safe. To reach him, Joab's army would be forced to destroy the entire city. Sheba found his refuge in the city of Abel, close to the northernmost border of Israel.

And he went through all the tribes of Israel unto Abel, and to Bethmaachah, and all the Berites: and they were gathered together, and went also after him. And they came and besieged him in Abel of Bethmaachah, and they cast up a bank against the city, and it stood in the trench: and all the people that were with Joab battered the wall, to throw it down.—2 SAMUEL 20:14–15

Imagine the terror reigning in the midst of the city. Sheba and his rebel army are occupying the city. Joab is leading David's army in besieging the city. They have surrounded the city walls and have begun to batter and tear down these fortifications.

In the midst of the city in particular, terror reigns. Perhaps Sheba urged his followers on, shouting at them to stand fast and fight. No doubt screams filled the air as helpless women and children fled for cover and feared for their lives.

I imagine that axes were being hit against the wall. Men were slamming battering rams (thick, heavy beams used to beat down the fortified doors of a walled city) against the strong fortress, yelling at its citizens. Sheba was inside. Battle was raging.

But wait. Listen. Do you hear something? A voice that penetrates the shouting and the destruction of the walls? Could it be the voice of a—*woman?* Her tone is not condescending or authoritative. It's not fearful or defeated. But something about her sincere cry makes you want to step a little closer to hear what she is saying.

> *Then cried a wise woman out of the city, Hear, hear; say, I pray you, unto Joab, Come near hither, that I may speak with thee.*
> —2 SAMUEL 20:16

Somewhere among this mass of terrified Abelites, a calm woman steps forward. In the middle of the craziness and confusion, a wise woman cries from the wall of the city. The Bible does not mention her name. Still, she stands in stark contrast to this chaotic scene and is used of God to change the outcome of a very bad situation.

How did Joab hear her over the sounds of fighting men and demolition? What was it about her that caused them to even pay attention to her? Somehow, maybe because of her demeanor or her urgency or her wisdom, she was able to get the attention of Joab, leader of David's army. And she asked him to come near to her.

This woman had two weapons that no one else seemed to possess at this moment.

She Understood the Problem

Wisdom involves seeing situations from God's perspective. It is knowing what is right, based on the principles of God's Word.

From the heartfelt cry of this woman, we learn that she understood the problem. She possessed the biblical wisdom described above. She saw this situation from a God-given perspective. As the psalmist David described, because the meditation of her heart was of understanding, the cry of her mouth was one of wisdom.

My mouth shall speak of wisdom; and the meditation of my heart shall be of understanding.—PSALM 49:3

When she heard the angry cries of battle, this wise woman could have run to her home to protect her family or her belongings. She could have acknowledged the battle that was raging but ignored everything but her own welfare. But avoiding a problem doesn't make it go away or get better. Burying our head in the sand when a difficult circumstance comes our way doesn't change the outcome. Furthermore, joining the senseless battle would only hasten the destruction of the city.

Instead of ignoring the problem or refusing to understand its implications on her city, she assessed the situation and understood the root issue: Sheba was rebelling, and Joab should be attacking *him*— not the entire population of Abel. She understood the seriousness of what was happening and realized that if no one took calculated action, the city would be destroyed.

Too often, we go through our lives putting Band-Aids on our problems without understanding the real dangers or root issues. We spend our energy fiercely attacking the results of our circumstances rather than thoroughly dealing with the root problem causing these circumstances.

We look around us and assess our problems only on the surface. We say: Society is out of control. My personal finances are a mess. My home is not peaceful. My children don't listen to me. My husband doesn't treat me right. My friend offended me.

But in all our difficulties, we fail to truly understand what is going on below the surface. Instead, we get caught up in the chaos of the moment. The result is that our circumstances only worsen—the bitterness grows stronger, the relationships become weaker, and we live in a continual state of frustration, denial, and turmoil.

Not the wise woman of Abel. She got it. With a godly perception, she looked past the battering rams and the combat and saw the rebellion of one man.

Understanding the problem, of course, is only the first step. Thankfully, this wise woman used her understanding to make a difference.

She Boldly Confronted the Problem

As a young girl, I was incredibly shy. Growing up with an abusive father, I became very good at hiding my feelings and avoiding any type of confrontation or disappointment from others. (Even today, though I enjoy good fellowship and conversation with all types of people, I still tend to avoid confrontation at any cost.)

When I was in the second grade, my family lived in Santa Cruz, California. The school I attended was located some distance from our house, and every day I had to ride the bus home from school. Usually my friend and I would hurry to catch the bus like the dutiful girls we were, but one day we decided to linger behind to enjoy extra play time with our friends. As a result of our dilly-dallying, we missed our bus.

Suddenly, I was faced with a choice. I could tell the teacher that I had missed my ride (and she would call my mom who would call my dad), or I could follow the suggestion of my friend. "Let's walk home," she said.

Walking home seemed like the best way to avoid confrontation with my parents and teachers, so I agreed, and we set off for the walk home.

At seven years of age, however, my friend and I were not entirely capable of making wise decisions. It wasn't long before we approached the train tracks on the bridge which spans the San Lorenzo River. Far below, the river surged, its waters splashing and foaming. But instead of turning back, we crossed the bridge—much of the way with no guardrail to keep us from a dangerous fall.

After several unexpected obstacles, we finally made it to my neighborhood well after the sun had set. When we came in sight of my house, we could see the blue-and-white lights of a police car whirling and spinning their colors across the garage doors. My mom had called the police (and I'm sure the fire department, the national guard, and anyone else she could think of), and my dad was out conducting his own search and rescue mission on the streets of Santa Cruz.

My fear to face confrontation had created even more problems, confusion, and attention than I would have ever wished.

Proverbs 10:13 says, "*In the lips of him that hath understanding wisdom is found....*" Because the wise woman understood the problem, she could boldly confront it. Fear may have filled her heart. Perhaps she trembled as she stepped beyond the safety of a barred door or cried out of a high window. But instead of giving in to fear, she spoke with true wisdom.

Consider the current problems in your life. Are you running from them? Are you avoiding them, burying them in the sand of busyness, laziness, or indulgence? Are you afraid of what might happen if you step out in courage to address them?

Determine in this moment to confront those problems in the boldness of God's wisdom. Commit to spending time in God's Word to gain His perspective and to then boldly act in accordance with the truths He reveals to you.

You have problems. God has solutions. So cry out, wise woman. Face those problems with godly courage and wisdom.

CHAPTER THREE

The Communication of a Wise Woman

I often look back on my college years with fond memories. I came to know Christ as a young girl after riding a church bus to Sunday school. But it wasn't until I graduated from high school that I really had the opportunity to forge close friendships with like-minded, Christ-honoring young people. I appreciated my singles department and the leaders who invested in me and helped me continue to grow in my relationship with the Lord.

Though I desired to attend Bible college, my dad (who did not know the Lord at the time) was strongly against the idea. When the day finally came that I could go with his blessing (years after high school graduation), I was thrilled! But I was still very much like the seven-year-old girl who crossed the scary train tracks to avoid a tense or awkward confrontation. I was the quiet type, not the outgoing, gifted communicator.

Even so, I embraced every aspect of Bible college, including the social events. And I was glad when a young man asked me to attend an upcoming banquet with him. You could say our evening together was enjoyable, but our personalities didn't quite click in the way we may have expected. As it turned out, the evening did have its share of awkward exchanges and minor miscommunications (probably largely due to my being quiet and shy).

When the night was over, though, I was still so thankful for the opportunity to have even gone on a date with a Christian young man. So I went to a store and purchased a simple but heartfelt thank you card.

The front of the card contained a beautiful picture with no words, and the inside simply read, "Thanks a lot!"

The minute I saw the card, I knew it was perfect. I saw those three words saying with elegant simplicity exactly what I wanted to say: "Thank you so much for wanting to give me a great evening." I jotted a short note, signed my name, and dropped the sealed envelope off at the campus mailroom.

I was surprised a few days later when the young man confronted me, obviously upset. He said he couldn't believe that someone as quiet as I could be so sarcastic and rude.

"What do you mean?" I asked, truly shocked that I had offended him.

"Your card said, 'Thanks a lot!' I know we didn't have the greatest evening, but you didn't have to rub it in by sarcastically saying 'thanks a lot' as if you meant, 'thanks for nothing!'"

I took the next several minutes trying to explain to him that I was truly very thankful and did not intend to come across as sarcastic in any way. What

a miscommunication! (I'm thankful that my next
date was with my future husband, and the rest of my
college dating experience continued on full of fun and
enjoyable conversations and memories.)

This experience hasn't been the only one over
the years that involved a lack of communication
skills on my part. But at least in retrospect, it is the
most humorous. The truth is wise communication
doesn't come easily for me, and I need God's help to
communicate like the wise woman in 2 Samuel 20.
In her example, we see two specific characteristics of
wise communication.

Speak Only to Those Who Are Part of the Solution

Many of the decisions I make in life are recurring—
embracing a healthy lifestyle, for instance. I choose
this often, mostly because I fail more often than I want
to admit. When I stray from healthy eating habits, the
Lord is not usually the first one I run to for help. Let's
just say that prayer isn't usually on my mind when

I'm sitting down with a gourmet cupcake (except for asking the Lord to bless it, which is a little ridiculous when you think about it).

My husband *definitely* isn't the first person I go to. He has many God-given gifts, but mercy-showing isn't his primary one. Though he would be the best person to help me with a solution and offer great accountability and motivation, I usually would rather have a sympathetic ear.

So, I gravitate to my friends who say, "Let's go out to eat and talk about it. You can start over again on Monday." Now that's what I like to hear! I'd much rather you be a part of my comfort than a part of my solution.

This wise woman in our story, however, went directly to the one man who was the hinge to the solution of her problem, even though going to him required leaving her comfort zone. Not only did she understand the root of the problem and take action to deal with it, but she took the only kind of action that could help—speaking directly to the man leading the battle. She called Joab out specifically. She didn't speak to the soldier with the battering ram. She didn't run to her city officials to have a council meeting. She didn't try to rationalize with Sheba. She went straight to the person directly related to the solution.

When problems arise in your life, decide that you will only go to those who can help you.

First, go to God. Ransack His Word for godly wisdom. Claim His promises to give wisdom to those who ask for it and seek it. (See Proverbs 2:1–6 and James 1:5.) The great thing about going to the Lord with your problems is that you get both comfort *and* solutions. (Now that's what I'm talking about!)

You may also go to a godly and trusted mentor, someone who has gained godly wisdom through experience. Perhaps this is your pastor's wife or another trusted influence.

In some cases, you may need to go directly to the person involved in the problem. In this wise woman's case, she had to confront Joab, and she had to do it in the midst of battle, perhaps while his hand was lifted to knock another brick out of her city wall.

...Hear, hear; say, I pray you, unto Joab, Come near hither, that I may speak with thee. And when he was come near unto her, the woman said, Art thou Joab? And he answered, I am he. Then she said unto him, Hear the words of thine handmaid. And he answered, I do hear.—2 SAMUEL 20:16–17

I like to try to imagine how the wise woman spoke to Joab. What did her tone sound like? She cried out, but I'm sure she wasn't rude or bossy. She referred to herself as a handmaid, which indicates a spirit of humility.

Read James 3:17 in light of the wise woman's example: "*But the wisdom that is from above is first pure, then peaceable, gentle, and easy to be intreated, full of mercy and good fruits, without partiality, and without hypocrisy.*" I think this verse accurately describes the manner and spirit in which the wise woman spoke to Joab. She was respectful, peaceful, and gentle.

You might be like me, nervous to approach anyone at all in anything resembling a confrontation. Or you might be the type to approach everyone and anyone who will listen. But no matter where you fall on the scale of willingness to communicate, make sure that your approach is full of the godly wisdom described above, and speak only to the one who can bring about a Christ-honoring solution.

Because the wise woman of Abel spoke with God-given wisdom, she was a voice of reason. And as strange and miraculous as it seems, Joab heard her voice above the noise and confusion and listened to her.

In the midst of difficulties, resist the urge to get emotional or caught up in the drama of the moment. As you share the right message to the right people in the power and wisdom of the Holy Spirit, He will use your voice to speak above the noise and confusion of your problem and direct your paths toward the solution.

Carefully Articulate the Problem

While we know that the wise woman had a good understanding of the real problem at hand, Joab and others in this story did not seem to have a similar grasp on the situation. Their perceived problems did not match the real problem.

Quite possibly, Joab assumed that the entire city of Abel was siding *with* Sheba and *against* King David. In Joab's mind, the city was protecting Sheba, so he would destroy Abel.

From the city's perspective, they perceived that Joab was against their city. Did this mean King David was against them? They may have thought, "Why is Joab, our ally, destroying our walls?"

Perhaps at this point in the story, you identify with Joab or the inhabitants of Abel. Maybe you have problems for which you've tried many solutions that have failed. It may be that you have misunderstood the nature of the problem. If you don't know what the real problem is, you can't find a solution.

The truth is, we all tend to be like Joab, making problems bigger than they need to be. Instead, ask God for the wisdom and grace this woman so obviously possessed. Notice her careful communication in the following verses:

> *Then she spake, saying, They were wont to speak in old time, saying, They shall surely ask counsel at Abel: and so they ended the matter. I am one of them that are peaceable and faithful in Israel: thou seekest to destroy a city and a mother in Israel: why wilt thou swallow up the inheritance of the LORD? And Joab answered and said, Far be it, far be it from me, that I should swallow up or destroy. The matter is not so: but a man of mount Ephraim, Sheba the son of Bichri by name, hath lifted up his hand against the king, even against David: deliver him only, and I will depart from the city.—2 SAMUEL 20:18–21*

The wise woman reminded Joab that her city was famous for its wisdom. She said that they had been known since the "old time" for their counsel in hard matters.

She also reminded Joab that the city of Abel was peaceful and faithful to King David and the God-appointed leadership of their nation. In addition, the Old Testament law stated that before attacking a fortified city, you would first have to offer terms of peace. If the inhabitants refused the offer, only then could you attack. Joab, in his zeal, had dug the trenches and started battering down the wall without thought to an offer of peace, which the city of Abel would have most likely accepted.

Then, she asked Joab why he was about to destroy part of the nation and more specifically, part of the inheritance of the Lord to His chosen people. By asking him, rather than accusing him, her words pricked his conscience rather than hardening his resolve.

Because of the carefully and calmly stated words of this woman, Joab stopped his charge against this city. Her words caused him to see for himself the real problem. It wasn't Abel. It was Sheba. In an effort to protect God's people, he actually was destroying them. He got caught up in the spirit and passion of the circumstance. While the wise woman had the composure to understand the problem, she also communicated it in a way that would speak to Joab's head and heart in the heat of the moment.

Perhaps your problem is sensitive. You feel like you are the wise woman, having sought for the wisdom of God, now crying out from your walled city. Around you is chaos, devastation, and confusion. Since biblical wisdom is having God's perspective *and* acting on it, now you must speak out in the wisdom of God.

If you're nervous, that's okay. I understand, because I am, too! I'm sure the wise woman was nervous as well, but God promises to give you the wisdom to speak words of grace, peace, and truth. Psalm 37:30 says, *"The mouth of the righteous speaketh wisdom, and his tongue talketh of judgment."*

Speaking words of wisdom requires courage. As you may have guessed, we can learn courage from the wise woman of Abel.

CHAPTER FOUR

The Courage of a Wise Woman

We stated in an earlier chapter that biblical wisdom can be defined as seeing things as God sees them—having a godly perspective of situations you face. But there is a secondary aspect to biblical wisdom. Wisdom is not simply having the knowledge to deal with problems in a capable manner. Instead, it involves viewing situations with God's perspective and responding the way God would want you to respond. Simply put, biblical wisdom involves *knowing* what is right and then *doing* what is right.

Many times, this is where we face real struggles in striving to be wise women. We know what to do, but we can't seem to find the courage to step out and actually accomplish what God has showed us to be His will.

From the example of the wise woman of Abel, we see three ways we can courageously demonstrate wisdom in our lives. Our story picks up after her communication with Joab.

Joab had assured this woman that if the city would hand over Sheba, he would lead the army to retreat. Now she had to convince the city that this was their best course of action.

> *Then the woman went unto all the people in her wisdom. And they cut off the head of Sheba the son of Bichri, and cast it out to Joab. And he blew a trumpet, and they retired from the city, every man to his tent. And Joab returned to Jerusalem unto the king.*
> —2 SAMUEL 20:22

How did this woman demonstrate courage? Furthermore, how can we?

Be a part of the solution.

This point is a little repetitive, but it bears another mention because our heroine was tenacious in being part of the solution. Not only did she call out to Joab, but she followed through in suggesting a solution to the people of the city.

We are reminded that she could have been a part of the problem. She could have quietly defended her home while people foolishly destroyed it. Instead, she not only cried out in the chaos, she chose to end the chaos.

It's always easier to be a part of the problem. We can quietly defend our position and stubbornly hold to our opinions while everything around us is destroyed, or we can courageously determine to be a part of the solution.

Is your walk with God not as strong as it once was? Choose to be a part of the solution by renewing your diligence in seeking God.

Is your spirit becoming frustrated, annoyed, bitter, or restless? Choose to be a part of the solution by yielding your spirit to God and applying His Word to your mind and heart.

Are you frustrated with God because He hasn't given you a husband? A child? A house? A position? A relationship? A possession? Choose to be a part of the solution by turning to God with a heart of trust.

Is your marriage struggling? Are you waiting for your husband to come to his senses and make things right? Choose to be a part of the solution by offering forgiveness first and showing love even when it's not immediately returned.

Are your children losing focus, lacking responsibility, becoming lazy, or needing direction? Choose to be a part of the solution by asking God for answers and renewing your commitment to applying them.

Are you tired of watching your community suffer from the effects of sin? Choose to be a part of the solution by sharing the love of Christ and the message of the gospel.

Do you have a friendship that is struggling or not spiritually edifying? Choose to be a part of the solution by seeking wisdom from God's Word and applying it to that relationship.

Don't let time and relationships and opportunities pass by while you complain about the problems surrounding you. Ask God for wisdom, study His Word, and then do what He has shown you to be right. Actively participate in righteous living, and enjoy the blessings of applying godly wisdom. It takes courage, but it is worth it.

Take Immediate Action

I find it easy to procrastinate. In fact, if I have an overwhelming or large project looming over me, I'll procrastinate to the point that I'll do almost *anything* other than confronting that task. I'll organize closets, clean out drawers, and do all kinds of things that aren't time sensitive or important.

This wise woman of Abel didn't hesitate or procrastinate. She got right to work. Joab told her to deliver Sheba, and deliver Sheba she did.

What a beautiful picture of submission, obedience, and teamwork. Joab and this woman held a mutual respect for each other. They also shared a mutual loyalty to King David and passion for loyalty in the kingdom. So, although Joab was grossly misguided in his actions, the woman pointed out their common ground and quickly worked to seize Joab's moment of understanding and willingness.

When we seek to apply godly wisdom to our lives, we will face opposition. We will continue to fight spiritual battles that require immediate action. Determine to stay alert and engaged. Be quick to obey the prompting of the Holy Spirit as you go through each day, and be willing to take immediate action when He reveals His will to you. Colossians 4:5 instructs, *"Walk in wisdom toward them that are without, redeeming the time."*

Work with God's People

Sometimes, in our quest to become women of wisdom, we begin to play the martyr. We see all of our problems and think we are the only one who is this busy, this stressed, this overwhelmed, this discouraged, this tired, this unappreciated, or this unimportant. We can easily adopt a "poor me" attitude as we seek to be problem solvers, refusing or overlooking help, support, or advice from those close to us.

It's probably not surprising to you at this point, that we see none of this spirit displayed in the life of the wise woman. On the contrary, when Joab requested that Sheba be thrown over the wall, the wise woman *"went unto all the people in her wisdom."* Sheba was surely surrounded by armed guards. There's no way this woman could have marched up to him, captured him, and delivered him to Joab alone. Instead, she asked help of and motivated the people around her. Together, they did what needed to be done.

God is so good to give us the support and encouragement of His people as we travel on this journey of life. As you search for wisdom and apply it to your life, remember that you are not alone. We are *all* on this treasure hunt for wisdom. Let's rally together, support each other, work together, and rejoice in victories together!

As you endeavor to step out in courageous wisdom, remember this woman. She was part of the solution, she took immediate action, and she worked together with God's people to see His will come to pass. May the same be said of you and me as we rightly respond to life's challenging situations.

CHAPTER FIVE

The Choices of a Wise Woman

The biblical account of the wise woman of Abel highlights our need for wisdom and demonstrates what it looks like when we apply wisdom to life situations.

But how did she become wise? For that matter, how do any of us gain wisdom?

The pursuit of wisdom is not only a worthy endeavor, as we've seen in this story, but it is attainable. Anyone who desires wisdom and is willing to make the choices required to gain it, can find it. We find these choices throughout God's Word.

Fear the Lord

Did you know that the primary source of wisdom is not a college classroom? (There are many educated fools.) It's not even the life experience gained through the school of hard knocks. (There are many experienced, but bitter, people.) Actually, the primary source of wisdom is the Lord Himself.

> *The fear of the LORD is the beginning of wisdom: and the knowledge of the holy is understanding.*—PROVERBS 9:10

To fear the Lord means to acknowledge His presence in your life and to live with an awareness that He is watching, guiding, and directing. As you seek to live in a continual awareness of God's presence, as you respect and reverence Him as your Lord, the Bible promises that you will gain wisdom. In fact, this principle is so foundational to receiving godly wisdom that the Bible says fearing the Lord is the *beginning* of wisdom.

Ask for Wisdom

Another way to receive God's wisdom is to simply ask for it! God promises to liberally, or freely, give wisdom to those who request it.

> *If any of you lack wisdom, let him ask of God, that giveth to all men liberally, and upbraideth not; and it shall be given him.*—JAMES 1:5

I love how this verse emphasizes God's graciousness. When we find ourselves asking God for wisdom, it's often because we realize that we've made a mess without it. And yet, for whatever reason we come to God asking for wisdom, He won't upbraid us—scold or reprimand us—for our lack. He won't make us feel badly for asking. He *wants* to give us His wisdom.

For the LORD giveth wisdom: out of his mouth cometh knowledge and understanding.
—PROVERBS 2:6

Search for Wisdom

Have you ever lost something important to you and searched desperately for it? Perhaps it was your keys or your phone or your pet. What actions do you take when you search for something of value? Do you passionately go after it? Do you lift up your voice and cry out for it?

What if someone gave you a modern-day treasure map in which "X" marked the spot of hidden treasures. Would you passionately pursue it?

That is how we must search for wisdom.

So that thou incline thine ear unto wisdom, and apply thine heart to understanding; Yea, if thou criest after knowledge, and liftest up thy voice for understanding; If thou seekest her as silver, and searchest for her as for hid treasures; Then shalt thou understand the fear

of the Lord, and find the knowledge of God.
—Proverbs 2:2–5

Wisdom is the principal thing; therefore get wisdom: and with all thy getting get understanding.—Proverbs 4:7

As we practice God's presence in our lives and ask Him for wisdom on a daily basis, we shouldn't neglect seeking His Word for the wisdom contained therein. We should study, meditate, and dwell on the wisdom that is from above.

One of the portions of Scripture with the most concentrated applications of wisdom is the Book of Proverbs. Thus, a practical way to search for wisdom is to read one chapter from Proverbs every day. Not only will this give you immediate wisdom to apply to your life, but over time, as you read and re-read these wisdom-rich chapters in Scripture, you will begin to develop a repository of God's wisdom in your heart that the Holy Spirit will bring to mind as you face various difficulties.

Stay Away from Fools

No matter how diligently we seek wisdom, if we spend significant amounts of time with foolish people, whatever wisdom we glean will be quickly neutralized by their influence.

Carefully consider the relationships in your life. Are you allowing influences that don't edify or encourage godly wisdom, but rather lead you into paths of foolishness and frustration? Scripture warns us to avoid these influences.

> *Enter not into the path of the wicked, and go not in the way of evil men. Avoid it, pass not by it, turn from it, and pass away.*
> —Proverbs 4:14–15

While we should demonstrate a heart of biblical love to all people, determine not to allow foolish influences to have entry into your life. Avoid foolish discussions, speculation, gossip, and counsel. Turn from it and pass away.

Furthermore, seek out relationships with people whose lives demonstrate the continual application of godly wisdom. By spending time with them, their wisdom actually will rub off on you!

> *He that walketh with wise men shall be wise:*
> *but a companion of fools shall be destroyed.*
> —PROVERBS 13:20

Tune Your Ears to Wisdom

Have you ever talked to someone and sensed that while she was *hearing* you, she was not *listening?* Sometimes we do this with God's wisdom. We let His Word, the preaching and teaching of it, and the counsel of others go in one ear and out the other.

Conversely, have you ever talked to someone in a crowded or noisy area and been gratified by seeing her leaning in to hear you? This is how we must listen to wisdom. God's wisdom is easily accessible, but we'll never gain it without inclining our ear or straining to listen to His still, small voice.

> *So that thou incline thine ear unto wisdom,*
> *and apply thine heart to understanding;*
> —PROVERBS 2:2

If you tune your heart to God's voice, His wisdom can be heard above the chaos and confusion. Lean in. Get a little closer to Him. Incline your ear. As you ask for wisdom and then listen, He speaks wisdom to your heart.

Develop Wisdom through Practice

After we pray for wisdom, seek wisdom, and tune our ears to hear God's wisdom, the time comes when we must act in God's wisdom.

> *Get wisdom, get understanding: forget it not;*
> *neither decline from the words of my mouth.*
> —Proverbs 4:5

Sometimes, we know what we should do, but we decline to do it. Perhaps God is leading us to do something hard or awkward or uncomfortable. But God's wisdom is not like a Pandora app or an ipod playlist in which you listen to your favorites and disregard everything else. God's wisdom may require that you take actions you'd rather not take. But do it anyway. Act in wisdom anyway. Allow God to bless you and increase your faith as you grow in your practice of godly wisdom.

These choices to gain wisdom are not always easy, and they don't come without competition. Although it sounds so simple to say, "Just ask God for wisdom," the truth is, in the moment when we most need wisdom, we usually have several other voices, including our own heart, pulling at us to act in fleshly wisdom. And as committed as we may be to reading a Proverb each day, we'll find 101 urgent needs calling for our attention at the very moment we planned to seek the wisdom found in God's Word.

Although God often gives us generous pieces of wisdom in our moments of desperation, the actions that make us truly wise women require earnest, tenacious, and repeated choices. If you're like me, you won't make the right choice every time. But God graciously helps us up when we fall and encourages us to go on in wisdom.

Over time, as we continue in the fear of the Lord, in asking Him for wisdom, in seeking it from the pages of His Word, in avoiding close relationships with those who lead us away from it, in tuning our ears to hear it, and in practicing its applications in our lives—as we make these choices again and again, God will increase His wisdom in our lives.

When Wisdom Abounds

My son Matt and daughter-in-law Katie live a few hours away from us, and we try to visit them as often as our busy schedules allow. A couple years ago, a group of family members jumped in the car and made the drive to Matt and Katie's around the time of our oldest grandson's birthday.

Camden was turning three, and his Uncle Matt and Aunt Katie promised him a special surprise when he got to their house. Sure enough, when we arrived, Katie had arranged the perfect treasure hunt for a three-year-old boy, complete with rhyming clues that he would understand, a map for him to follow, and a box full of treasure waiting for him at the end of the hunt.

The treasure hunt was designed for Camden, but I noticed about halfway through that we *all* went on the treasure hunt with him. As we walked through the neighborhood, we were joyfully encouraging his progress and cheering at the discovery of each new clue. When he found the treasure box, we all rejoiced as if we had discovered true treasure.

Proverbs 3:13 tells us that this is what it looks like when wisdom abounds—happy. *"Happy is the man that findeth wisdom, and the man that getteth understanding."* It is the complete opposite of what it looks like when folly reigns. In place of chaos, loss, and distraction, there is peace, happiness, and joy.

While not every situation is particularly exciting or exhilarating, and while you may not have a team of people cheering you on when you make a wise choice, the internal joy and peace that fills your heart when you find and apply God's wisdom is incomparable.

We started this booklet describing the effects of folly, but let me encourage you with the results of wisdom. When you find and apply wisdom, God promises happiness and prosperity. Peace and joy. Calmness and sensibility.

I pray that as you close this little book and continue your day, that you will be determined to be a wise woman that God can use. As you cuddle your baby, go to work, sit at a desk, pray with a teenager, love your husband, and serve your God, may you do so with wisdom that is from above. And may you experience the joy and happiness that God promises as a result.

This is my prayer for you—that you will commit to search for and apply God's wisdom.

 TERRIE CHAPPELL has served joyfully and faithfully by her husband's side for over thirty years. For twenty-nine of those years, she has supported her husband, Paul Chappell, as he has pastored Lancaster Baptist Church in Lancaster, California. God has given them four children who are all married and serving the Lord in Christian ministry. They also have eight grandchildren.

You can connect with Mrs. Chappell through her blog terriechappell.com.

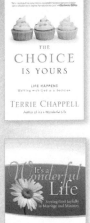

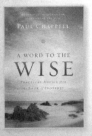

Visit us online

strivingtogether.com

wcbc.edu